REACH!

from single mom on welfare to digital entrepreneur

Lorraine C. Ladish

#WEALLGROW '16

You deserve a BREAK.

Lorraine

Table of Contents

To every kindred soul who has been a part of this leg of my journey.

You know who you are.

When Things Go Wrong

When things go wrong, as they sometimes will,

When the road you're trudging seems all uphill,

When the funds are low and the debts are high,

And you want to smile, but you have to sigh,

When care is pressing you down a bit,

Rest, if you must—but don't you quit.

Life is queer with its twists and turns,

As every one of us sometimes learns,

And many a fellow turns about

When he might have won had he stuck it out.

Don't give up, though the pace seems slow—

You might succeed with another blow.

Often the goal is nearer than

It seems to a faint and faltering man.

Often the struggler has given up

When he might have captured the victor's cup.

And he learned too late, when the night slipped down,

How close he was to the golden crown.

Success is failure turned inside out—

The silver tint of the clouds of doubt—

And you never can tell how close you are.

It may be near when it seems afar,

So stick to the fight when you're hardest hit—

It's when things seem worst that you mustn't quit

—Edgar A. Guest (1881-1959)

FOREWORD

"When you stand and share your story in an empowering way, your story will heal you and your story will heal somebody else." – Iyanla Vanzant

WE ALL LOVE SUCCESS STORIES, tales of overcoming adversity and finding wealth and happiness, like the one about a Michigan farm boy named Henry Ford, or the dyslexic child who became Sir Richard Branson, or that college dropout, Steve Jobs. When we think of success stories, we often look at stories of massive financial wealth. But not all of us have that image of success. Many of us envision success as simply living life on our own terms. Doing it, as Sinatra sang, "my way". Not everyone is ready to embark on this type of journey because society at large doesn't seem to agree with this concept of "making it".

And then there is the myth that success – however you choose to define it – is a straight shot upwards, when in reality the path is filled with peaks and valleys. Missing the mark, taking a detour or a wrong turn, and failure—yes, failure—are all a part of our life's journey.

The sooner we realize that our current circumstances, whatever they may be, don't define us, the better. That way, when we're in dire straits, we will know in our heart that this is not forever. And when we're riding the wave of fulfillment, we will also not rest on our laurels, because this too, is temporary.

We all face challenges of different types, and I've had my fair share of them since childhood. But I've also had wonderful triumphs and beautiful breathtaking moments. That's just life. One day you get good news and maybe a few hours later tragedy strikes.

My first book, written when I was 29 and published when I was 30, dealt with a grueling eating disorder that had a tremendous impact on my life. After publishing that book, I realized that what came easiest to me was writing about things I had first-hand experience with. And this became my purpose in life. Despite having a vocation I loved, earning an income and working on my own terms, the best thing of all was receiving a letter from someone in a faraway country telling me my words had touched their life in a positive way. This still fills me with gratitude and joy on any given day. It rocks my world and gives me the energy to tell others: *this is how I traveled this leg of the journey of life and hopefully it will inspire you to find your path through the mist.*

So now that I'm 52, I find that I once again have a story begging to be shared. Because I know I'm not the only woman who's been through divorce, unemployment, poverty and depression. I weathered all of this as a single mom of two young girls, when I was in my mid-forties. But the story I'm about to tell you could apply to any woman of any age, at any stage of her life, with or without children.

This is the story of how I woke up one day to find myself broke—both financially and emotionally. I was completely helpless. And how in the span of five years, I reinvented myself from being an unemployed writer to a well-paid online communicator and influencer. But the most important part of it all is how I leveraged my skills to build my own online business, Viva Fifty Media LLC. In its first year, my website Viva Fifty! was not only profitable, it supported our family of five. In the first twelve months I made the figure that apparently guarantees happiness and well-being. They say that any amount above that – according to the experts – does not make one happier, although that remains to be seen!

I've told bits and pieces of this particular part of my journey in blogs and in speaking engagements. But I have never told the entire story in detail—until now. I hope it resonates, and that in it you can find something that may inspire you to roll up your sleeves and get to work and make things happen for you, especially when the going gets tough.

I thank you from the bottom of my heart for reading this story. While I still keep a diary for cathartic purposes, this writing is for you. I hope that you too find success—whatever this might mean for you—and that you might pay it forward to others who could use a hand during difficult times.

Warmly,

Lorraine

Sarasota, Florida. 20th of November, 2015.

CHAPTER 1

The Year I Lost Everything

"It's only after we've lost everything that we're free to do anything." — Chuck Palahniuk, Fight Club

TODAY MY PEERS KNOW ME as a successful online influencer. And by successful I mean that I make a full-time living online. That was not always the case. Supporting a family of five with my online business, Viva Fifty Media didn't happen overnight. It was a journey that started in 2008, the year I lost everything.

In late 2008 and early 2009, I found myself the unemployed single mom to two young girls ages 4 and 7. This was hardly the ideal situation for a 45-year-old woman who couldn't find work in her area of expertise: writing and translating. But the Great Recession was only the catalyst for something that should have perhaps happened years earlier: my divorce.

Although that played a huge part in forcing me to reinvent myself, I place no blame on others for any of what I am about to tell you. And I know I'm not the only woman who has faced what seem insurmountable challenges. We all confront problems big and small—sometimes on a daily basis. That's life, after all. But it's what we do when we come upon these roadblocks that makes a difference.

My marriage had ended long before I moved out with my girls. I think both my husband at the time and I knew that. But being children of divorce ourselves, we did everything possible to make our relationship work. We tried a trial separation, spent over two years in marriage counseling, attended self-improvement retreats, and practiced forgiveness. None of that saved our relationship as a couple. Yet it did one thing: it helped me realize there was nothing left but to break away and start again—solo.

To give you an idea of how much I just wanted to get out of the relationship and move on, I took nothing when I left except clothes, books, my laptop and a box with my family's heirloom jewelry. All I needed was to be with my girls. I also wanted them to have their dad close by, so I didn't go far. When I filed for divorce I didn't hire a lawyer, and neither did he. We represented ourselves and decided together on the custody arrangements. We weren't going to let anyone else make that decision for us. We parted ways as a couple but not as parents.

My ex-husband and I had moved to the U.S. together in 2004, with our two babies. Before that we had been living in Seville, Spain since 1998, when we were married. He worked as a civil engineer. I was a simultaneous interpreter, a translator and an author. Together we made a decent living. But my husband wanted to pursue new opportunities in the United States, and I decided to support his decision. Unfortunately, our move to Florida was somewhat traumatic for me. I found myself alone with my daughters in a gated community in the suburbs without a car. There is just no way of getting around in certain places of Florida if you don't have wheels. There aren't even sidewalks to walk on if you wanted to, or public transportation for that matter. My husband spent his days at work for the first few months while I tried to find my footing in our new home.

In the beginning I raised our daughters at home and continued writing books that were published in Spain, but there was a problem: I wasn't in Spain to promote them. Pretty soon I realized that wasn't going to work. I needed to establish myself in Florida, where I knew no one and no one knew me. I had to start over. I reached out to local newspapers. In a couple of months I was interviewed by *La Palma*, a now defunct Spanish supplement of the *Palm Beach Post*. Soon after, I offered myself as a writer for them. That marked the beginning of my writing career in the U.S. Pretty soon I was writing three articles a week for La Palma. I also wrote for other Hispanic publications, and got translating gigs with book publishers.

My family and I eventually moved away from the small town of Port Saint Lucie, Florida. My husband was laid off from his first job in a matter of a few months and we struggled to stay afloat while he job hunted. Eventually we relocated to Naples, Florida, again for my husband's work.

On the outside, to other people, things looked terrific. We were living in a beautiful house close to the beach. I worked from home as I've always done. My husband was Project Manager of a luxury homebuilder. Our children were beautiful, healthy and happy. But on the inside we were struggling to keep our marriage going, leading very lonely and separate lives. Our daughters were our only common ground.

When the recession hit, both my husband and I found ourselves unemployed. He lost his job, and I was out of the regular gigs I'd been working on for the past few years. We quickly ran out of savings and racked up a ton of debt.

That's when everything cracked. Our marriage finally fell apart.

The reasons for the break-up, like all break-ups, are complicated and not the fault of a single event or of either my ex-husband or myself. Also, his story is not mine to tell, so I will leave out the details of our irreconcilable differences. What matters is that it happened. And it's during the aftermath of this personal storm where this story really begins.

One of the hardest things of being bicultural is having your family and friends far away. When I announced my separation, my dad told me to return to Spain, where his side of the family lives. But I didn't want my girls to be away from their father. Moving back was not an option. With the help of my sister, who lives in San Francisco, I rented a small apartment. My grandmother in

Spain sent me a little money from her pension every month.

I started looking for work, but the boom was over. Newspapers and magazines weren't hiring. As a matter of fact, La Palma closed down, as did many other newspapers and magazines. Book publishers had their translations budgets slashed. Even worse, I was in the epicenter of the bust. As the economy collapsed, Florida was one of the states hardest hit because of its reliance on real estate and development as an economic engine. Things were bad. And I was soon to find out just how bad.

When I couldn't find work in my field, I switched gears. Forget a career, I needed to make money, period. Every day I went out and applied to all kinds of jobs: cashier, warehouse worker, sales clerk, restaurant server. But I got turned down at each and every place. I had no experience in those fields. And I was 45 years old. On top of that I had to find something where I could manage my children's schedule. How would I take care of them after school if I had to be at a job?

Creditors called non-stop. The repo man came to my door to try and take my car while the girls and I were at home. I broke down crying more than once, feeling like a terrible mother. Things were spiraling out of control. I had nothing. I couldn't even see a light at the end of the tunnel. I was desperate.

I was no stranger to depression. It runs in my family. When I was alone and the girls were with their father, there were days I just couldn't get out of bed. I'd wake up feeling pressure against my chest. I felt like my body was made of lead. All I could do was cry myself back to sleep. I was exhausted all the time, like I'd been in a bad car accident or had some other physical ailment. When the girls came back from being with their dad, I would put on my happy face and do my best to enjoy my time with them.

I was wiped out. I had nothing—literally. I couldn't afford cable so I piggybacked off of the neighbor's unsecured wireless connection for Internet access. I was living on rice and beans and the kids on mac and cheese. There were many evenings when my girls would play with the kids next door and stay for dinner. One day, my neighbor asked me to please join them. Apparently my daughters had mentioned to her that our refrigerator was always empty. I will be forever grateful to than Rumanian mom.

A few days later I mentioned this to a good friend. He asked why I hadn't applied for food stamps. I dismissed him, saying, "They're for poor people."

He just looked at me and raised an eyebrow. That's when I realized I was poor.

That same night, using the neighbor's Internet connection, I Googled "food stamps", and applied.

My daughters came with me to the welfare office to turn in certain documents. When the girls asked me what the place was, I tried to be vague. I said they helped people like us, who may be having a little bit of a difficult time. I looked around the office and I saw desperation in other mothers' faces; women who waited nervously, just like me, to hear their name called. Their children were, like mine, happily playing or reading magazines, oblivious to the dire straits all of us were going through.

The feeling of relief I felt when I received the card in the mail a few weeks later, is something words cannot convey. I would be able to get food for both my daughters. I had not applied for assistance for myself.

For the first time in months we went grocery shopping. The joy I saw on their faces when I allowed them to pick a treat was priceless. I will never forget that afternoon as we trudged up the stairs to our apartment with grocery bags filled with cereal, milk and real food I could cook for lunch and dinner. It felt better than Christmas.

But for me, the best part was knowing that no matter what, for the next six months at least I'd be able to feed my little girls. The knot in my stomach finally let up, even if just a bit.

But stress takes its toll on the body. I'd had a root canal a year before but I'd never been able to get a crown because I couldn't afford it. I was clenching my jaw in my sleep from the stress. One day, the tooth cracked. It abscessed and needed to be extracted, but I couldn't afford it. I was in terrible pain. All I could do was take over-the-counter painkillers just to make it through the day.

At night I watched my children sleep. Their closed eyes, their calm breathing, relaxed bodies, their innocence... I didn't want them to lose that.

I'm not a religious person, although I was raised as a Catholic in Spain. I do believe in a Higher Power, in something bigger and more powerful and wise than all of us. There were many nights when I would kneel down at the end of my bed and look up at the ceiling, and say out loud, "Please tell me what to do." I felt utterly and hopelessly powerless. Then, I surrendered to that feeling.

Self-reflection tools

No matter where you are in life now, think of difficulties you have faced and overcome in the past. If you did it then, you can do it again—no matter what is thrown your way. I learned early on in life that struggles and challenges are what shape our character. They make or break us. And the way we handle them determines to a large extent how the rest of our life will unfold.

If your struggles are happening in the present, I humbly suggest that before trying to overcome them, you strive to embrace the mess. Feel the sorrow, the frustration the pain, the hopelessness. Only then will you be able to fully surrender and realize that once you hit bottom, the only way to go is up.

One of the things that helped me through these tough times was letting go of anger and resentment. After years of my husband and I pointing fingers at each other it was time to stop blaming someone else. I was just as responsible for cornering myself into a big financial and personal mess. But I also felt like I was undergoing a phenomenal transformation at every level. Physically, emotionally and spiritually. I realized nothing mattered more than my children's and my emotional well-being. And that was being taken care of.

Exercises

- Write down a list of challenges and difficulties you have overcome in the past. Reflect on how they shaped who you are today.
- Enumerate any and all struggles you are enduring at the moment. What can you learn from them and what steps can you take to blast through them.
- What physical activity can you practice that is free that will help you stay centered during critical times.
- Elaborate on resentments, grudges and anger that you harbor towards people or situations. It's important to acknowledge these before you can really let go and move on.

- Consider that in order to move forward sometimes a clean break is necessary. In relationships, business and work. Can you do this?
- What kind of help do you need, and whom could you ask? Sometimes moral support is enough to help us get through hard times.
- Keep a running list of compliments people give you, so you can reread when you're not feeling good about yourself.

CHAPTER 2

Opening Windows When Doors Were Closed

"We have to continually be jumping off cliffs and developing our wings on the way down." — Kurt Vonnegut

DESPITE GETTING TURNED DOWN for jobs one after another, I refused to give up. I had to move forward. I had to find something. I had to pay rent and put food on the table. I kept thinking something would have to turn up. It just had to. It was a question of odds. If I kept trying it would happen. Even when I was in the grip of depression, I looked for work. And then when I felt I had knocked on every door in Naples, I turned to other alternatives to bring in money.

This is how I fell into direct sales.

A friend of a friend introduced me to a skin-care line that seemed decent enough. My best friend helped me pay for the samples and kits and I got started peddling the creams. It wasn't easy. To be honest, sales are not my forté. And with a product I was lukewarm about, it was really, really hard. I soon realized this was not going to work out. I figured direct sales was a good idea, but skin-care was just not the right product for me. I was losing time, energy and money.

Shortly after, at one of my skin-care parties I met a fabulous lady who sold silver jewelry out of a catalog. I love jewelry. Despite my failure selling creams, I felt confident I could be successful with the jewelry. So my best friend once again loaned me money for catalogues and samples, and I wore the jewelry everywhere I went. Women would compliment me on a necklace or a bracelet and that made it easier to sell. But I couldn't rely entirely on strangers purchasing my goods.

One of the hardest things for me was making phone calls to get prospective clients to host a jewelry party for me. These are events where friends get together and a sales rep, in this case me, shows the bling and hopes the guests will buy it. Sounding uppity and positive and taking rejection after rejection is not easy when you're broke and your next meal depends on someone saying yes. It's almost impossible not to sound desperate. I'm pretty sure that nobody who saw me selling jewelry—oftentimes with my daughters in tow—would imagine that I was dying inside every time someone said they would not place an order.

Every afternoon when my daughters would go play at the neighbor's apartment, I'd cry for a few minutes before picking up the phone and making those dreaded calls. I was terrified of hearing the word "no". I set up a photo of my little girls at the table so I could look at them while I made the calls. Then I took a deep breath and made as many phone calls as fast as I could to get through my list. It was painful. But guess what? I did get some direct sales parties, at least enough to help me pay a good chunk of bills. But selling jewelry was not my salvation—far from it. I just barely squeaked by each month. The food stamps helped tremendously. And while things were a little better, those were difficult times. What I didn't realize at the time was that writing would once again pull me through this dark period.

In 2006 I had started a blog for no other reason than to try a new form of writing. It didn't have a specific purpose or focus. But in 2008-2009 I renamed it *Success*

Diaries. I also wrote it in Spanish, as *Diario del éxito.* My posts were short bilingual entries meant to keep myself in a positive frame of mind. I was also sure there were other women out there hit hard by the recession, going through a divorce, maybe battling an illness. Perhaps my weekly reflections could help others.

I wrote and posted on the blog every week, no matter what. I didn't know it then, but this was my first incursion into the online world that would eventually help me reinvent myself. That blog was kept at the most unsuccessful time of my life. But I found a purpose for it that helped me stay strong and see glimmers of hope sometimes.

We tend to think of success as this really huge word that embodies large accomplishments like fame and fortune. But in that blog, which is still online, I wrote about the small successes of life. But back then for me, success was simply mustering the courage to get out of bed and face my reality. I wanted others to realize that success comes in many small ways that eventually add up.

I knew that I had to win the fight—for me, but also for my girls. I realized that I had to focus on the tiny little triumphs of each day. They gave me hope. I took on a variety of daily practices to keep myself grateful even for the simplest things like cooking dinner and enjoying time with my daughters. Every morning and every night I wrote in a journal. Sometimes I would pour out my feelings to sort myself out. But the main purpose of this diary was something entirely different. I decided early on that would be the place where every day I would find things to be grateful for. I knew I could rewire myself back into a positive state of mind.

Sometimes my gratitude list was very simple:

The cashier was nice to me.

The girls' teachers gave them new socks.

I found a lucky penny in my pocket.

I had enough gas to take the girls to school.

We went to a free movie night.

I still have that journal. Keeping a gratitude list is a part of my daily routine even today. No matter how busy I get, I always find time to write and be thankful for what I have. I don't want to ever forget to say *thank you* for the good stuff.

A couple of years after I started *Success Diaries*, I pitched the blog as a book to my agent in Spain. I needed the advance money. And although it was not a big advance, every little bit helped. A year later, in 2012, the book *Diario del éxito* was released in Spanish.

Another practice that helped me stay grounded during those desperate times was one that I'd picked up when I was young and recovering from an eating disorder. I had a glass jar, an old powder box that had belonged to my deceased grandmother. Whenever a worry or a fear took hold of me, I would write it down on a small piece of paper. Then I would fold it and put it in the jar. I called it my *God Jar*, and my intention was to let go of my worry by turning it over to a Higher Power.

This is what some of my concerns looked like:

I'm scared I will be evicted next month.

I'm worried I will never find a source of steady income.

I'm afraid that I won't be able to write another book.

What if my children stop loving me?

What if I fall sick and can't see a doctor?

Once a month I would go to my jar and unfold all those small pieces of paper and read them. If my concern was something I no longer harbored in my heart, or hadn't materialized, I would throw it away. If it was unresolved, it would put it back in the jar. Years later my eldest followed that same practice and she says it also helped her overcome worry and fear. When I asked her what she could possibly have been worried about, she said that she wanted me to find a job and that a friend at school had given her money and hoped she wouldn't get in trouble.

Aside from reading books that I borrowed from the library, such as *Welcome to my Crisis, A Course in Miracles, Dark Nights of the Soul, The Four Agreements,* and many more, I took up another practice to help me stay positive. My girls and I would collect pebbles at the park. When we got home, with a sharpie I wrote words on them. They were mostly feelings, both happy and sad: *sorrow, sadness, desperation* and *hopelessness*, but there was also *joy, hope, calm, peace* and *quiet*. Every night I would choose the pebbles that reflected my feelings for the day. Sometimes there were a lot more sad than happy feelings. But other times, joy won out. This simple routine was a little like keeping a Zen garden that helped me visualize what I was feeling. The best part about it was to see that there were some good days, even though it felt like the world was crashing down on me.

All of my life, since I was very young, I found that sports, running, exercise and dance, helped me alleviate stress. I was a fitness instructor in my twenties and I took up modern dance as a hobby well into my thirties. I loved it.

So while I was trying to piece my life back together as a broke, unemployed single mom, I turned to what had worked in the past. In the afternoons and on weekends, I would take my daughters to a nearby playground. While they had their fun, I would run in circles until I felt the endorphins kick in.

It was about this time that one of my best friends dragged me to LA-style Salsa classes. It was crazy. We had to drive 45 minutes to another city to attend the classes. I wasn't always in the mood, but once I was out on that dance floor learning new moves, I forgot about my troubles. Some nights I would take my children with me. Other times they stayed with their dad. They now remember those evenings fondly. I have videos on

YouTube where you can see me practicing moves while my girls are running around the studio with other kids.

One of my main problems is that even when I'm running or working out I can still entertain all kinds of neurotic thoughts and drive myself crazy. But when I'm dancing, because I have to focus on the rhythm and on preparing for the next step, there is no room for thinking. When I dance, I don't have a care in the world. I'm truly in the flow, joyful and happy. Salsa dancing became my therapy.

Something else that helped me hang on to threads of hope back then was that during my worst times, I discovered the goodness in people. It took me a while to realize I was truly a person in need. Food stamps, the local charity food ministries, and the girls' school were all a godsend. But I received many acts of kindness with the utmost gratitude and humility. Some of those include:

My children's school administrator knew what I was going through and put my family on the charity list for Christmas. One Saturday in December of 2009, volunteers of the charity surprised us at our little apartment with a huge bag filled with wrapped toys and clothes for my girls, and a gift card to buy Christmas dinner. I welled up in tears as I hugged those cheerful and kind volunteers. Now I make a point of donating to children in need every Christmas season. I know what it's like to be on the receiving end.

The teachers and the nurse at the school gave my girls gently used school uniforms and new underwear, socks and tennis shoes.

When I had nothing. When I had no food in the fridge and was so depressed I couldn't get out of bed, one of my friends showed up unannounced with bags of groceries.

There were times when my friends would take me out to dinner and drinks knowing there was no way I could pay my way.

A songwriter I met through MySpace composed a song for me. It's called *Take a Chance.*

An acquaintance put me in touch with a dentist who extracted my abscessed tooth for free. He prescribed antibiotics as well. I was missing a tooth but my health was on the mend.

The moms of kids at school would host jewelry parties for me where I sold my jewelry. They didn't have to, but they did. I will never forget each and every one of them.

As I write this, my heart sings again, realizing how angels who tread this earth carried my girls and me along when I was too tired and depressed to carry myself. To this day, I still believe in the kindness of strangers. The next chapter is the story of how one particular unexpected act of kindness propelled me to get out of my rut.

Self-reflection tools

I know first-hand that it is not easy to see solutions when we are surrounded by problems. But there are things we can do to rewire our brain to find hope and to renew our faith and recover our energy.

The things I did to keep myself going in a dire situation may not be for everyone. But they worked for me. I encourage you to try them and even come up with your own. Whatever stage of life you are going through now, know it can—and probably will—get better. Time will go by whether you practice gratitude or not. Time will pass if you look for those windows of opportunity and the clock will continue to tick if you don't. Experience tells me it's better to fake it till you make it than to wallow in desperation. It's okay, and perhaps even part of the healing process, to wallow for a bit. But there comes a point when you have to take action. Little by little you will notice that the gratitude practices will start to seep into your soul. It will all come together and you will eventually spread your wings and fly. The power of practicing daily gratitude is huge. Do not underestimate it.

Exercises

- The first thing that may go out the window if you're going through a crisis is self-care. Make sure you make time for self-pampering. And don't let anyone tell you it's frivolous.
- If you can't afford it, try to barter services. Maybe you can get a good haircut in exchange for writing the copy for a stylist's webpage.
- Don't let pride get in the way. Life has a way of leveling out. If you allow for others to lend you a hand, you will very likely be in a position to return the favor or pay it forward in the future. It's all an energy cycle. Karma.
- Be mindful of little gestures of kindness. Even when you're feeling down, tune in to other people's positive energy. Be open to it.
- Keep a gratitude journal and write in it every single day. Even if you think you have nothing to be grateful for. You will find something. Maybe the

feel of the sun on your face in the morning, a warm cup of coffee, the smile on a stranger's face.

- Keep a God or worry jar or box. Write down your concerns and fears and close the lid on them. Every week, open the jar and see what happened with these doubts.

CHAPTER 3

The Act of Kindness That Changed My Life

"No one is useless in this world who lightens the burdens of another." — Charles Dickens

ONE OF THE BIGGEST TAKEAWAYS from my year of hardship was that every challenge brings with it moments of intense joy. I don't buy into the stereotype that the world at large is out to trip you up. There are kind people who will offer you help at the most unlikely times. And that was my biggest lesson.

I told this story for the first time onstage at a blogging and social media conference. I had never even blogged about it because I had promised my benefactor that I would keep it to myself. But as time went by and I got back on my feet, I knew I had to spread the news even if I kept my friend's identity anonymous. After I told it in public for the first time, I found her online—we had lost touch after I had moved away—and I once again thanked her for that act of kindness.

During that unbelievably hard year, even with my small income from direct sales, help from family and welfare, there were a number of times I almost didn't make the rent. One of those times, the landlord threatened to evict us.

I couldn't ask friends and family for more money. They had done as much as they could. Those were tough times in general.

One night as I kneeled down by the foot of my bed, asking for guidance, I saw a solution. The box with my family's heirloom jewelry. I went to my closet and opened it.

These pieces of jewelry were the connection to my past, the one thing that I felt I carried with me from my country of birth—my family's heritage. In the box was the ring my grandfather wore the day he died. Another gem belonged to my great-great grandmother, which she wore in a picture that hung on my grandfather's office wall while I was growing up. There were also a number of pieces of jewelry my *abuelita* had given me over the years because, she said, she didn't want to wait to be dead to bequeath it. There was also my own wedding ring, and gifts for my daughters, given to them by family and friends when they were born. All these items held great sentimental value for me. I had always hoped to pass them on to my children.

I studied the contents of the jewelry box. I touched the jewels and thought of their history and remembered the stories behind each piece. I cried.

That night I emailed my dad in Spain and told him what I was going to do the next day: find a jeweler and sell the gold by weight so I could pay my rent. My grandmother gave me her blessing. She told my dad to relay to me that she'd given those jewels to me for a reason. And now I needed to sell them.

The next day I visited a local jeweler I had met a year earlier at a networking event. I showed him my pieces and asked him how much I could get. What I thought would be a relatively fast transaction turned into long, heart-wrenching hours. He had to test, weigh, photograph and itemize each piece. He needed to pull out the gems from the rings. As I handed over each of the pieces of my family's legacy, I felt my heart bleed a little. My youngest, then 5, was with me. She had no idea what was going on. Her eyes sparkled as she admired the jewelry at the store with her little nose pressed against the display window. She said those were beautiful jewels princesses wore.

When every piece of jewelry I handed over was accounted for, the jeweler cut me a check. He mentioned it would be worth more if I exchanged them for new pieces from his store. But I needed the cash. My most prized possessions turned out to be worth exactly a month's rent.

My heart dropped when I exited the store. But then my little girl held my hand tight as we walked towards the car. When she looked up at me and smiled, I knew I'd done the right thing.

I deposited the check and paid the rent the very next day.

One Friday night a few weeks later, toward the end of the dance class I attended, one of the regulars—a schoolteacher—invited me to have a bite to eat. She knew why I attended dance classes. Most of us had a reason to attend the dance lessons. It usually had to do with escaping daily life. I was no different.

We sat at a booth at a restaurant and she asked me how I was doing. I calmly told her of my situation and how I'd been forced to sell my family's jewelry to pay rent.

"Did they pay you good money for them?" she asked.

I had no idea, but they had kept a roof over my head. "It was just enough to pay the rent."

We continued chatting about life, her work, my children. It was almost midnight when she picked up the bill and said, "I have something for you. And I'd love to give it to you tonight."

I had never been to her house. Our point of connection was the dance studio and, as much as I liked her, we'd never hung out outside that environment.

I hesitated. She insisted.

And so I followed her through neighborhoods I had never been to. It was dark and I wasn't quite sure where I was. Some of the areas we passed were questionable—the kind of places I hoped my car wouldn't break down at. I wondered what I was doing. Was I being rational? But something inside me told me to keep going.

We arrived at her house. She asked me to sit down in the living room. Then she disappeared into her bedroom. A moment later she came back holding something.

She placed it in my hands and wrapped her fingers around my fists. When she let go, I looked down. There were two sets of engagement and wedding rings from her two failed marriages.

"I was waiting for the right person to give them to," she said. "And it's you."

I was speechless.

"Please take them, and sell them. For your girls."

I cannot begin to explain the amazing wave of gratitude that washed over my soul.

And for my girls, I did.

I was so very grateful that I wanted everyone to know what a wonderful person she was. I mean, she was a schoolteacher with a humble income, a woman who had suffered huge heartbreak in her life. And she was doing this for me.

I mentioned that I would post it on Facebook. I wanted her to know that I would publicly acknowledge her incredible gift.

But then she said something I will never forget: "Esto queda entre Dios, tú y yo." (This is between God, you and me.)

I cried all the way home. But they were tears of joy. Indeed, there were good people in this world. Here was someone who believed in me perhaps even more than I did. Someone who thought I was worthy of her help.

The next day I again visited the jeweler, and once again I got a check. Next month's rent was paid for. My kids and I would be all right.

That single act of kindness had such a profound impact on me, I knew I would do everything in my power to climb out of the darkness I'd been living in. It wasn't so much the jewelry or that I had enough to pay the rent for the next month. It was the gift. It was the trust and belief she had in me. It wasn't charity. It was help. And I was going to make the best of this gift. I knew then that I would find a way to move forward and out into the light.

That event taught me one of the most important lessons in my life: my family's legacy was not really in that box of jewelry. I keep those memories in my heart, and I will pass them on to my children by telling them the stories of the past. It's also the reason I don't wear gold anymore. Instead I wear the kind of silver jewelry I used to sell in direct sales as a reminder that every struggle in life indeed has a silver lining. But the most important lesson I learned from this was that women do help other women, that Latinas help other Latinas.

Ever since then, I make it a point to lend a helping hand if it's within my reach. I know that even behind the widest of smiles there could be an aching heart. I'm by no means a saint. But whenever I have the opportunity, I pay it forward.

Self-reflection tools

There seems to be a widespread notion that women don't help other women. That people are essentially evil. That it's a jungle out there. I'm not naïve. I know there are mean-spirited people. There are human beings with twisted intentions. I hear it from friends and colleagues. We see it on the news every day. Trust is thwarted, lies are told. Too many people hurt other people—even people they love.

But the opposite is also true.

If you are going through a difficult time, avoid being whiny but let people know what's going on in your life. You never know who is in a position to lend you a hand.

And if you are on the upswing, look around you, dig beneath the surface and find out whether a colleague, a friend or even someone you only see at the gym, may need a little help.

Helping others is really the gift that keeps giving.

Exercises

- Look back at your list of grudges, anger and resentment. Start to practice forgiveness, starting with yourself. Forgive yourself for anything you feel guilty of. Perhaps you feel it is your fault that you are struggling.

- Forgive others whom you believe have wronged or hurt you. Remember that any tie—financial or otherwise—is still a tie. If you have to argue with someone to get something from them (an ex-spouse for example), ask yourself whether it's worth your time and energy. It's almost always better to cast out ballast and move on. You will feel lighter on your journey.

- Money comes and goes. I know it's a tough pill to swallow when you can't pay the bills or are struggling to make ends meet. But it's true. Maybe right now someone else needs it more than you do.

- If you're at a good point in life, tune in to those around you and see whom you can help. You will feel much better and perhaps help restore their faith in people.

CHAPTER 4

Reinventing Myself Online

"It's never too late to be what you might have been."

— George Elliot

TODAY, MY ONLINE BUSINESS Viva Fifty! Media supports my family of five. My current husband (more on him later), who is also a writer, is my business partner. This is today, now. But I never want to forget how or why I got here. And I also want to always be aware that any kind of success is not a destination but a journey. I don't know what the road ahead has in store for me, but I will never forget the path that brought me to this point in time.

I firmly believe that in order to climb out of an unfortunate situation one has to be open to opportunity, however small it might appear. We must saddle up and ride it—see where it leads. Pride should not get in the way. By allowing yourself to put your skills to work in new ways, you just might be surprised where it may take you.

Dancing at a studio during those bleak days did more for me than just help me socialize and forget my daily burdens. It also opened windows of opportunity—a combination of face-to-face interaction and a little help from social media. I had opened a MySpace account in 2007, when a younger friend insisted I use the social media platform to promote my books and connect with other creatives. I was a little reluctant at first, but in the end I did open an account. That's where I met great colleagues, writers, editors, creatives, some which I call friends today. During my journalism days I also used MySpace to find interesting people to interview for the newspaper. I kept a blog there too, which had no other purpose but to unravel my thoughts and perhaps entertain. In early 2008 my sister, who lived in San Francisco, urged me to join Facebook. Once again I was reluctant, but I did it anyway. For a while I kept a foot in both social media platforms. I connected with most of my dancing acquaintances on both sites.

Then one day, while dancing at the studio, a young businessman—the kind that just knows how to orchestrate a good hustle—told me he'd noticed my profile. He needed a writer and thought he could use my services. That's when I got my first online gig. The deal we agreed on was that I would write around forty 300-word blog posts each month for his online coupon site. The posts would not have my name and I would get $12 per post. I would be paid twice a month. Right now that might seem like very little money—peanuts, really. But for a broke mother who's behind on her rent and needs to feed her kids, $480 a month was a godsend. It wasn't my kind of writing, but it was writing. And I could work from home. The job was right up my alley. The only catch was that I had to make the posts "SEO friendly". I had no idea what search engine optimization was. My new client gave me a quick overview of what it was and how it worked. The next day I started pumping out those posts like my life depended on it. And it kind of did.

I will be forever grateful for that serendipitous request. There I was, an author with fifteen published books, an experienced journalist, ghostwriting tedious blog posts that were not exactly soul lifting. But I did it.

And I did it with great pleasure. Every two weeks I ripped open the envelope with the check and smiled all the way to the bank to make a deposit.

A month later, I forced myself to attend a networking event in Naples, Florida, where I met a website developer. I explained how I was writing SEO-friendly posts for a website. He told me he built websites, but didn't want to write the copy. Within a couple of weeks he started sending clients my way. I would interview them about their business and wrote the copy for their site. I got paid $20 an hour for writing about anything: kitchen cabinets, bathroom remodeling, dental procedures, tree pruning services, you name it. It wasn't my passion, and my name wasn't anywhere on the copy. But I was writing for money!

In order to better serve my clients I started researching how to write for the Internet and write proper SEO. I felt a new window of opportunity had opened for me and wanted to take full advantage of it. Newspapers and magazines weren't hiring, but this Internet business was paying my bills. I wanted to learn everything I could about the new media.

My clients seemed happy with my work, but most importantly, my income grew. So things were getting better, but I didn't want to rely on these two clients. So every now and then I would reach out to past clients, in case there had been a change in their budget. One day, an editor who I had worked with when Babycenter en español first launched, gave me the happy news that they had given her a budget for my freelancing services. I wrote several articles and translated quite a bit of content for the site. After two long years of desperation, I felt like I was back in the saddle.

Of course, freelancing (something I've done my entire life) has its ups and downs. When you're on top of your game it's great because you can manage your cash flow and prepare for the months when you don't have as much work. But when you're starting afresh, it's not so easy. Every penny counts, and a slow month can put you back where you started from.

In the meantime, a journalist from Spain who I also met online introduced me to the editors in charge of the blog section of the Spanish magazine HOLA! I started posting the Spanish version of my Success Diaries blog on their site. HOLA! didn't pay, but I was already writing the content for my own blog, and the exposure was tremendous.   I met a lot of new people—writers and editors.

One month, when work was almost at a standstill, another colleague, who I'd met when I interviewed her years back for La Palma, sent me a lead: About.com—which at the time belonged to the New York Times—was looking for writers for their new Spanish website. I checked out the available subjects and applied to a couple of them: Literature and Tips for Moms. If I got the gig, it would mean $675 a month for quite a bit of work: eight articles, eight blog posts and a weekly newsletter. But to me it meant a steady income. That was enough to fuel my passion.

When I got the email letting me know I had been selected—along with a number of other writers—to try-out for the Tips for Moms (Consejos de mamá) section, I was thrilled. Except the selection process would take—get this—four weeks!

There was no time or energy to celebrate. In the first two weeks, all the selected writers would be creating content. Those who passed this section of the test would go on to actually populate the site.

Needless to say, I worked my butt off. It wasn't just about posting the content, I immersed myself in how to fine-tune SEO and other best practices for writing for the web. I was teaching myself as I went. I also had to complete the work for my other clients while I did that.

When the two weeks were up, I received the good news that I would go on to phase two of the selection process. That meant I would be creating a mock website. To give you an idea of how little I knew about that, I didn't even know what the term "back end" meant. I had never even seen a website on the inside other than Blogger, which is what I used for my personal blog and is incredibly simple and user friendly.

All this was new to me. But so was that steady paycheck. I needed this. I wanted it so bad I could taste it. So once again, I dove into the Internet and researched "back end". And let me tell you, it's no picnic. I had to learn basic HTML to manage the About.com site. One day I broke down crying. I didn't know what I was doing. I was certain that I was going to mess it all up. I recall another contender for one of the About.com sites telling me that she'd given up because the back end was so difficult. I wasn't going to give up. So I read all the documentation, watched dozens of tutorial videos. I took my own photos, sized them up and posted content. To this day I still believe that was one of the biggest tech challenges I had ever faced. But I did it. I finished my site and turned it in on time. I was so exhausted and relieved to be done with it, I figured that if I didn't get the gig, at least I'd learned a heck of a lot of new skills in a very short time.

I waited for what felt like the longest week of my life. When I received the email letting me know I'd gotten the gig, I cried. I mean I really cried. $675 dollars a month. Writing. Online. I couldn't believe it.

But that was just the beginning.

Working for About.com taught me a lot about online ethics. Because it belonged to the New York Times, the same journalistic ethics applied to me. I learned everything about disclosures when reviewing products, conflicts of interest, and so much more.

Offering tips to Latina moms was a subject I cared deeply about. I was a mom. I had written books about parenting. And I had worked for Babycenter. For the first time since I had been working as a journalist for La Palma, I was writing what I wanted to write. And I had a byline. Every article I wrote for Consejos de mamá had my name on it. I put my heart and soul into that page. You would think I was being paid ten times as much. But I wanted to make a difference, and I wanted to keep learning.

With the About.com site, writers also get paid a certain bonus or royalty when their number of clicks are above a certain base figure. This meant more money. It was great motivation.

That's when I started my first Twitter account. When I tweeted links to my blog, my page views would go up. But I didn't really understand Twitter, nor did I make a huge effort to. I didn't have the time or mind to explore it. At least, not yet.

A few months after I settled into this About.com gig, a new website for Latina moms popped up. It was in English and was called Mamiverse.com. Recently I had been introduced to the Editor-in-Chief at the time. I contacted the editor and pitched a few stories. Pretty soon I was writing four or five posts a week for them. The pay was pretty good, and between that, About.com and a couple of other gigs, I was finally making enough money to pay the bills with a little left over for savings.

In the meantime, a book I had written earlier, *Volver a empesar*, about finding love again in midlife, was published in Spain. I contacted the Miami Bureau Chief of the Spanish news agency EFE whom I had met at an event back in the days when I worked at La Palma. The agency ran a great article about my book a few weeks later. And that was that.

A few months later, I received an email from him asking me what I was up to these days. I explained about all the online work I was doing. He told me he was taking a leave of absence from EFE to launch a news site for Hispanics, in English, called VOXXI.com. He asked me my rate. By then I had already dropped the $12 blog posts for the coupon site and was concentrating on clients that paid on average about $250 a post. As we ended our conversation, I agreed to write a couple of articles for VOXXI, which was set to launch in November of 2011.

A few days after I'd turned in my articles to VOXXI, he called and asked about my online following. At the time I had exactly 700 Twitter followers. I had a lot more page views when I combined all of the outlets I wrote for. Then he invited me to travel to Miami for a meeting about how I could collaborate with this new site. As I drove the three and a half hour drive from Sarasota to Miami, I wondered what might be a good price to charge just in case his intention was to offer me a weekly column.

I was impressed by the VOXXI offices in Coral Gables. I met the staff and we had a productive meeting. Then we went out to a nice Spanish restaurant in the neighborhood. In the end I was offered something very different: editor of the Lifestyle section. I was so shocked that I didn't know what to say. I didn't even know whether I wanted to be an editor. I always saw myself as a writer. I had so many questions: could I work remotely, would the job be task-based, would I have a schedule. How much was the pay?

One week later I accepted their offer.

I drove down to Miami and spent a few days at the office learning the ropes. That's when I realized that with my short experience working online, I had more knowledge about how to run a web-publication than anyone else on the team. They were great professionals from print media, from large corporations. This was an online startup.

It was also a news site. So the pace was fast. I put together my own team of writers, hired a copy-editor and ran with it. In under a year I learned a ton about planning a publishing schedule and leading a team of contributors. But also that office politics can suck the life out of you—even when you're not physically in the office.

At VOXXI I met great people. I learned that I could create and lead a team and obtain excellent results. I also learned that I wasn't cut out for that type of fast-paced cut-throat environment.

As things turned out, right when I was getting ready to leave my position at VOXXI, the Editor in Chief of Mamiverse let me know she was leaving the company. Her position was vacant. She said I was rocking the online world and I was a mom—I'd be perfect for it. I didn't waste any time. I reached out to the owner of the site. A few days later, over lunch in Miami, we shook hands and I became the new Editor in Chief of Mamiverse.

I loved that website. It was the perfect place for me, as a Latina and as a mom. It was as if everything else had led to this moment. I was still a contractor. I've always been self-employed, and I stress this because it's in my nature. Even after everything I went through after my separation and unemployment, I don't believe there is such a thing as job security. Besides, I always wanted to know that I was my own boss, that my so-called employers were in fact my clients.

For two years, I proudly represented the site, led a team of writers and the production team. I treated the publication as if it was my own. I wrote editorials, organized Twitter parties, did blogger outreach, social media activations and so many other things I hadn't done before. I had wonderful mentors who helped me along the way. I will forever be grateful for their help and support. I earned a decent salary and had enough work on my plate, so early on while at Mamiverse, I left About.com, the site that taught me so much and started my online career as a mom blogger.

Leading a website that for a time was acclaimed by the Latino community was a wonderful and enriching experience. It took me to places and gave me experiences for my family and me that I wouldn't have had otherwise enjoyed. Of course, it also came with long hours, many challenges and the stress of responsibility.

I made it my mission to keep myself relevant, to be a compassionate leader and manager. I wanted to serve the readers and the community as well as my colleagues.

I spoke at social media and blogging conferences. I did my best to keep up with the latest online trends. I made a great effort to make a difference in the Latino community.

I couldn't believe it. Two and a half years after hitting rock bottom, I was making a decent living doing something I loved. I was managing a site that served women just like me. In the middle of all this professional growth, I also met my soulmate. Life was pretty damn good.

Self-reflection tools

The bottom line of my story is that I learned to use traits I already had: persistence, resilience, a questioning mind, readiness to learn and my writing skills, in a different medium. Had I continued to try and make it in print I may still be in the same predicament as in 2009.

But because I opened myself to new media, new challenges, new platforms, I was able to leverage my skills, build on them and make myself marketable again.

If you don't like where you are professionally, if you would like to change careers, or if you are unemployed, I challenge you to ask yourself: How can I put my skills to work in a new way? How can I learn new skills that would make me more marketable?

Exercises

- In order to move forward in your career, or move in a different direction, write down all the skills and talents you have.
- How can you repurpose those skills or sharpen them to make yourself more marketable?
- What character traits do you need to develop in order to move forward? If you have lots of talent but don't have resilience or persistence, then you need to work on the latter.
- If you're burned out or really down and out, make a list of services you could offer based on your skills.
- Seek out mentors. Don't do it by whining. Let them know what your goals are and ask them to help you brainstorm ways of making money and moving forward. Listen, process, act.

CHAPTER 5

Launching My Own Platform, Viva Fifty!

"Create a definite plan for carrying out your desire and begin at once, whether you are ready or not, to put this plan into action." — Napoleon Hill

I TURNED 50 IN AUGUST OF 2013 and felt strongly about stating my age publicly. Conversations with peers and colleagues taught me that women are scared, not only of aging, but of ageism. Some women in their forties and even thirties would not disclose their age because they felt (perhaps rightly so) that they wouldn't get the assignment, the man, the job. They also confessed to being in crisis. At 50, I found myself in the best shape of my entire life physically, emotionally and professionally.

Things were also pretty good on the personal front. At 46 I had met the man I knew was a perfect fit for me. He is a former photojournalist, a writer, an artist, and like me, he's bilingual and multicultural. His son is similar in age to my girls. But more important is that he was also on a journey of reinvention. As a matter of fact, we first met when I was barely starting to climb out of my lowest point. He stood by me through my comeback, up until today and hopefully for many years to come.

We got engaged in front of our children in October of 2013, after four years together. I wanted to let other women know that yes, it's possible to find love again after a certain age. Yes, it's possible to climb out of the darkest nights. Yes, it's possible to reinvent yourself at any age. Yes, it's possible to peak after 50.

Meanwhile, as much as I loved what I was brought on to do at Mamiverse, things were changing. I learned that investors and advertisers ultimately drive the direction a business needs to follow. As the mission and purpose of the website evolved into something different from its original focus, I no longer felt passionate about my work there. My purpose of making a difference and helping Latina mothers felt stifled.

In January of 2014, after some soul-searching, I decided to launch a personal blog. This time, it was backed with the knowledge and skills I had acquired in the past few years. I wanted to create a site that portrayed my bilingual and bicultural background and that would reflect celebrating life at 50+. But to start a new blog I needed a good name. I knew that was crucial. It had to embody everything I was about and be catchy. Then one day during my morning run, I hit on it. That's how VivaFifty.com was born. I immediately registered the domain and started writing in wordpress.com. At the time it was only a creative and inspirational outlet.

I still gave everything I had to Mamiverse, and wrote on my new Viva Fifty! blog only a couple times a week, in English or Spanish, but the CEO of Mamiverse was afraid I would get distracted with my blog. It went well for the first few months, but honestly, as the direction of Mamiverse changed, I found myself getting more and more pleasure out of my own writing on VivaFifty.com. I regained the passion I once felt of delivering a message of empowerment and inspiration. I was once again, following my heart, my mission of delivering hope.

I think we both knew it had been a great ride for us as a team and also that it was over. It was time for both sides to move on. So in April 2014, right after I returned from a speaking engagement at Hispanicize, the Latino social media conference in Miami, and a week before my wedding to the love of my life, I took a leap of faith and parted ways with Mamiverse.

I had the wedding of my dreams: a simple ceremony at the beach with only our close family. With my hair down and bare feet in the sand, I said, "I do" to the man who is not only my husband but also my best friend and business partner. After the wedding, we spent our weekend honeymoon at a hotel on Sanibel Island and talked about what to do about Viva Fifty!. I would either seek another opportunity as the editor of another online publication, or I would go full throttle with VivaFifty.com. At the time I was also having a conversation with the publisher of a large project for Latinas. My concern was that if I became engaged in that particular venture, I might not have the time and energy to move forward with Viva Fifty!. We decided to move as fast as we could to get Viva Fifty! off the ground.

My goal was to have at least 100 posts in the site by the end of a month. We worked day and night to populate the site. My husband, my father, my sister and I all wrote articles and edited one another. I also reached out to a handful of fabulous writers I had worked with in the past, both in English and Spanish. By the end of the month we had surpassed our goals. Viva Fifty! was starting to take shape. It looked like a real magazine.

After working with large websites, I knew that the biggest downfall is having huge overheads. I was lucky. I had no investors and no staff, and had acquired the skills to handle it all myself. I built the social media following, created and edited posts, translated, chose and sized the photos, fine-tuned the SEO.

My husband helped me migrate the site to Wordpress.org and in the meantime I commissioned a logo that he had drawn for me on the back of a napkin during our honeymoon. That was our largest expense.

My initial investment was of around $1000, to include hosting, logo creation, stock photography and a little bit for content. The rest was sweat equity. I didn't have any seed money and I also anticipated that it would probably take at least a year to monetize the site. But I was wrong. I started getting requests for sponsored content the same month that I soft launched. The money wasn't enough to make a full-time living, so while I built the community, gained pageviews and expanded our social media reach, I also wrote for other outlets.

I reached out to colleagues, fellow editors. A week later I was writing for different sites like Latinamom.me. It was a great feeling to know that we'd managed to be friends even when working for competitive companies. I also started blogging again on Babycenter en español, for their new initiative Spanglish Mamis. Online friends and colleagues either gave me writing gigs or told me the doors were open.

I also took a temporary job as assistant managing editor at Mamás Latinas, of Café Mom. It was only a three-month stint while the editor was on maternity leave. And boy, was that a challenge. I had to manage half a dozen writers daily. I edited 20 posts a day and followed a schedule (something that's against my nature) from 8am to 6pm. I still wrote for other outlets. But most important was that every night I worked on Viva Fifty! Looking back on those three months, I have no idea how I pulled it off. Actually, I take it back. I do. I had the full support of my husband, who took over all the household duties while teaching at a local college and helping me with Viva Fifty!

But still, it was hard. And yet, after having gone through hell a few years earlier, I knew I had something that would keep me moving forward: Grit.

Six months after the soft launch of Viva Fifty!, I landed my first real sponsor for a one-year brand ambassadorship. They found me online and wanted to reach my demographic. I will never forget how, when I asked whether they wanted my media kit, they said: "No, we've looked you up, we know who you are."

I was floored.

As soon as I finished the Café Mom gig in December of 2014, I reached out to all the PRs and colleagues in my address book. This brought me another long-term activation that was a great fit for the site. I also joined blogger networks. I run my site more like a magazine than a blog, with publication calendars and contributors. I spent hours each week strategizing my social media reach. As my influence grew, the paid opportunities rolled in.

As a business, one of the best things about Viva Fifty! was that I actually had a very strong and specific niche: women over 50 (my strongest readership are women between 48 and 64), who speak English, Spanish, or both. During that first year I didn't have time to go find clients. They found me.

In January of 2015 my husband and I established Viva Fifty Media LLC. In April 2015, we celebrated the first year of the website. At that time, with the work I had secured for 2015, we had already replaced my income as Editor in Chief of Mamiverse. The best part of this was that I didn't have a boss. But I did have to be accountable to readers and clients. Still, I could choose what clients to say yes to, and this was a huge deal.

Considering I bootstrapped it, I am in awe of what vision, determination and hard work can do. In little more than a year, I achieved a considerable online following: a combined reach of over 150,000 followers across several social media platforms and 100,000 unique monthly visitors on the webpage. I always have my latest numbers on my media kit at **LorraineCLadish.com** if you are curious.

None of that came easy, especially because I deal with both a very specific audience and a bilingual site. It's hard to pull off a bilingual scenario because not everyone enjoys that aspect. But hey, that's what I want to do and the readers who like that, well, they tag along.

Today, all the different aspects of Viva Fifty Media and my personal brand as an influencer, fully support our family of 5. But I couldn't do this if we weren't a team. My husband takes care of the financial aspect and works as the editor in chief. He also writes fiction and teaches writing at a local college. He cooks dinner most nights, while I'm hosting or co-hosting Twitter parties or meeting deadlines. And the kids all help out testing products, posing for photos and doing their chores. Even our dog, Toby, has gotten in on the action by participating in videos and photo shoots.

It's not over yet. I don't think I've 'made it' and can now lie down and rest. Beyond my family I now have a small team that helps me maintain a quality website. I have someone who helps me with IT issues, loading posts and scheduling social media. I have go-to writers and contributors. I do the engagement and the personal and live posts. So yes, it's always me who responds to a tweet or a comment!

I still try and keep my monthly costs low. As I said, huge overheads have killed more than one website. Investors can change the direction of a site as their goal is to make a profit on their investment. I had a vision, to run my own website, one that had integrity and quality, and that would be helpful and empower women in my age group.

In my mind I'm just a hustler with grit and determination. I did what it took to follow through with my vision. When I look back at those first $12 posts for the coupon site I did back in 2009, I realize how far I've come. And when someone tells me: "Sending out a few tweets is only a few minutes of your time", my reply is that they're not paying me for my time sending a tweet, they're paying me for the years of work it took me to build the following they want to reach with those tweets.

I've been able to let go of smaller projects that clutter my mind and pay less than my average rate. I also feel that by doing that, I'm making room for people who are in need of those smaller projects, just as I was in need of them at one point in my life.

I continue to write for outlets I enjoy writing for. One of them is the Purple Clover, a website for people of a certain age that still feel young. Most recently, I've been contributing to the Huffington Post. A site that I once thought would be the ultimate outlet to write for.

The years of hard work now allow me to command larger figures for what I do—from writing posts, to social media activations, to shooting videos. I've set my rates based on the quality of my work and reach, and I take no less. Because I've worked hard for this and both my family and I deserve to be paid my worth.

That said—and against the grain—I still do work for free. For whom and why? For causes I believe in, for women who are starting their own businesses with the same grit and passion I put into mine. For friends and colleagues I feel a strong connection with. If I see determination and doggedness, I lend a hand in making those dreams come true. I have little patience for whining and negativity. No, I'm not positive all the time (just ask my husband). There are days when I want to disconnect from it all and spend the rest of my life on a desert island with no Internet. Online can get overwhelming sometimes. Other days, it's an absolute pleasure. I enjoy hopping on Periscope to share a bit of my journey, give tips on social media or write articles about subjects people often ask me about. That is extremely gratifying.

Despite the hard days when a lot of the work feels like a grind, I'm grateful. I'm extremely appreciative of the hard times, now behind me, and for all the work I did to climb out of them. I'm grateful for the people that gave me opportunities, for the women who helped me and continue to do so. The list is so long that it would fill an entire book. I'm happy that I can be at the helm of my own project, which was created with the vision to empower other women. To help them overcome the fear of aging, to inform them of the changes they can expect in their mind and body. To give them a place to connect with others who also want to thrive in midlife and beyond.

I aim to inspire. Although I need money to support the family, and a check in the mail feels great, the most rewarding aspect of my journey is when I realize I've touched someone. An email from a reader responding to my newsletter—which I try to make personal—a message from someone giving me leads to stories that pertain to my readership, a note letting me know a woman challenged herself to take a step in the direction of her dreams. All that fills me with joy, with purpose and even more determination to keep going. It's the reason I started writing books when I was much younger.

Is this the end of the story? Is this success? I'll let you know in the next chapter.

Self-reflection tools

What is your dream project? What could you do in the next 5-10 years that is worth investing your time and perhaps even money into? What is stopping you from doing it? In some cases it's possible to keep a day job that will enable you to fund your dream project. If you think you don't have time, think again. Nobody has time. We make the time. Also remember, that life is a journey. Maybe for a few months, or even years, you will need to work round the clock. But then there will come a time when you can reap the fruits of your labor and indulge in other pursuits that nourish your soul. For me, it was a matter of taking the plunge. Some of us are more successful in a sink or swim situation. I suppose I belong to the latter.

Exercises

- Some people really thrive on pursuing their dreams and doing what it takes to achieve them. Others love the IDEA of pursuing their dreams but won't do the legwork. You can train yourself to be the former.

- What is your dream project for the next 5-10 years? You can always course-correct later, but it helps to know your destination in order to map out your way there.

- What are you willing to do every day that will get you to where you want to be? Show up and do it even when it feels like nobody is watching. Do it even when you don't see immediate results. You rarely will. But time will pass whether you do this or not. So, do it and avoid living a life of regret.

- Start before you think you're ready. If you wait for the perfect moment to have a baby, to get married or divorced, to start writing a book, to launch your business, you won't do it.

- Seek out like-minded people to bounce ideas off of and for accountability. Don't let anyone drag you down. Surround yourself with go-getters.

- Put blinders on and don't waste time shooting the breeze. Sometimes in life you have to make certain sacrifices, or choices, in order to achieve what you really want. If I had gone to every party I was ever invited to, I would not have written all those books. I also would not have built my business.

- Be competitive only with yourself. There is enough work and money to go around. Do the best you can do, be the best you can be. And if you can't take on a client or a project, pass it on.

CHAPTER 6

Staying Grounded and Open to Affluence

"What you seek is seeking you." — Rumi

AS I MENTIONED AT THE BEGINNING of this book, many have the notion that success means achieving million-dollar status. There are dozens, if not hundreds or thousands of books about how to attain that kind of success. And while self-made millionaires prove this is possible, in reality it's a very small percentage of the population that tries and actually achieves such a level of fame and fortune. Furthermore, that may not be the kind of success you're after. I'm not saying I'd turn down a million-dollar offer, what I mean is that being a millionaire is not my ultimate goal.

My father, who I absolutely adore, and who is a linguist and lexicographer, means well when he tells me: "I know you will make it!"

My recent answer to him was, "But I *have* made it!"

I'm not being cocky with this. I believe I've made it in the sense that I'm living life on my own terms doing what I love to do. For my entire life, I've been a freelancer or self-employed. I started working part-time at 15 and full-time at 18. I didn't finish college due to an eating disorder, which took me years to overcome. That's a lot of years of never having a regular job. Sure, I did things I didn't enjoy here and there, but they were short-lived. It's in my nature to hustle to find a way out of the dark tunnel. I've also reinvented myself a number of times. I have dipped my toes in different fields that eventually converged to help me be successful in what I do today.

Among the many different hats I have worn at different stages of my professional life are: language teacher, fitness instructor, dance instructor, simultaneous language interpreter, translator, writer, journalist, producer, script adaptor for dubbing studios, book author, TV commentator. My hobbies include running, dancing, yoga, drawing, painting and dreaming that I could be a rock star or play the piano in my next life. Now that I run my own website, I've discovered my love for photography and video. I am incredibly restless. I want to do so many different things that I can't sit still. There are times I feel inspired to design jewelry, other times I want to design a line of clothing, or open a bookstore or a restaurant. So many things...

And yet, I know I have to rein in my dreams. I need to put my real skills to use, and relegate other aspirations to a creative outlet in my free time. I need to pursue more of what I do well and drop those things I'm not so good at. I've heard this said many times and it works wonders for me.

As you can see, my story is not a traditional full-blown rags to riches one. It's no fairy tale. But in hindsight, even as I was writing what you just read, I was amazed at everything that had to happen in the last few years only to arrive at the place I am today.

Supporting a family of five with your business in its first year is no small feat. We don't have a lavish lifestyle, but we are rich in the things that matter. I still work from home—as I've done all my life. I can take a day off whenever I want and then work on the weekend if I prefer. I can get up late (I am not a morning person). I'm always available for my children's school events. I live close to the beach so I can take a stroll by the shore when

I need to unwind. And that is something that no corporate benefits package can give you. I don't believe in job security. I think in today's economy that idea is a myth. I've seen too many of my friends and colleagues laid off, fired or simply let go in order to maximize profits for the stockholders of a large corporation. But I also know from experience that I'm only as good as my last gig—my latest blog post, contract, book, you name it.

At my age (52 at the time of this writing), I know that this is not the end of the journey. It's simply a milestone that I will strive to surpass. But at this stage I no longer feel I need to prove myself to anyone. A lifetime of different achievements—both personal and professional—have given me the confidence that if tomorrow everything I have today disappeared, I am equipped to see it through and reinvent myself yet again.

I'm also hyper aware of how lucky I am to have met a partner with whom I have a symbiotic relationship. We connect at so many different levels that it would be hard for me to do what I do without his support. And I know I've influenced his writing career, cheering him on and telling him not to take on certain jobs that would have hindered his productivity as a writer. Phillippe

Diederich, my life and business partner, recently published his first novel, *Sofrito,* with Cinco Puntos Press and his second book, *Playing for the Devil's Fire* is coming out in 2016.

We're able to have sit-down family dinners together and enjoy time with our children. Sure, we work a lot, but that work is exactly what we love doing. Most of the time it doesn't even feel like work, but just as an extension of our life.

I believe that one of the greatest benefits of running your own business is freedom—freedom of choice, freedom of time, freedom of work. My husband and I place our priorities in the things that we believe matter most to us. We don't drive new cars, or dress in designer clothes or eat out at fancy restaurants, but this past summer my youngest traveled to Spain on her own, the two eldest went to San Francisco, and my husband and I went to the mountains in North Carolina to an artist retreat. He taught photography while I took yoga and drawing classes, and wrote this e-book. Then he traveled to Haiti to see his family and I went to Chicago with my girls for a good friend's wedding.

I'm also at that stage in life where I've become very aware of my own mortality. I have good friends who are battling cancer, in some cases the disease has been diagnosed as terminal. An acquaintance recently lost her twenty-something-year-old son to a car accident. My mother had a stroke at 28. This is perhaps my biggest fear, that I could suffer a stroke at any moment. I recently ended up in the ER because of a kidney issue. I'm going through menopause and being very public about it via Viva Fifty! and on social media, to raise awareness. I have to have breast ultrasounds every four months, because the doctor found something in my breast that needs monitoring. Only a year ago, my children and their dad were in a rollover car accident that totaled the car. No one was injured, but it could have been fatal. My father, a fit and otherwise healthy man in his mid-seventies, underwent a quadruple bypass in February. My sister's best friend, the person who got her clean and sober—20 years and going strong—passed away in January. And more recently my sister's husband asked her for a divorce. Now I can be there for her and tell her there is life after a painful separation.

All this means I know that life can change at any moment. And because of that, I try to make time each day to pursue something meaningful. I still keep a gratitude list. I run, dance and practice yoga. I set aside pockets of time to be with my children, although it never seems like enough. I try to call my family in Spain regularly.

But I still make plans for the future. I believe in evolution, in progress. Now I'm considering my next logical step. One of those steps was to finally put this journey down on paper and share it with others. Those difficult years were very traumatic for me. I will never make light of them. I learned so much about myself, and it gave me an opportunity to look deep inside me and see exactly who I am. While I've written a blog post here and there and shared a few anecdotes about my journey while speaking onstage at a conference, I had never told the full story. I suppose I had to get some distance between in order to look at things with the proper perspective. It is only now that I feel comfortable with telling it. It is now that I can tell other women: yes, you trip and you fall and you recover. Yes, you can quit your job. Yes, you can reinvent yourself. Yes, you can find love again. Yes, you can do whatever it is you really want to do if you set your mind to it, and work hard for it.

Maybe you won't become a millionaire, maybe you will. But before you embark on your journey, ask yourself whether that should be your goal. Define your concept of success and then go for it.

I don't know what the future will bring, but I still have a bucket list of things I want to accomplish. I have a rough draft of a novel, a fun chick-lit story. I'm planning a product line of the tools that I used to help keep myself afloat when I was struggling. I'm launching limited editions of Viva Fifty! jewelry, and mapping out my next non-fiction books.

I'm reevaluating the direction of Viva Fifty Media and my personal brand to see how I can better serve my readers, followers and the Hispanic community I'm so fortunate to be a part of.

Will I do Viva Sixty!? Maybe. Maybe not.

Maybe I'll do something else. But one thing is certain, I will continue reading books on business, on art, on inspiration. I will continue to learn new skills. I will continue to stay curious and open to this turbulent and fantastic thing we call life.

And I will continue to practice visualization. It has helped me do what it takes to achieve my goals. When something works, stick with it.

When I was writing my first book at 29, I made a mock cover of the book, and posted it in several key places in the house. I looked at it when I took writing breaks and when I had dinner and when I pedaled on my stationary bicycle. I had it by my mirror in the bathroom. That kept my fingers writing every day until the book was finished. I got creative and hustled to secure a publisher. But there would have been no book to publish if I hadn't done the groundwork.

I still envision the goals I want to attain. I can see myself sharing my story of reinvention over and over. I can see myself helping other women reach their goals. I can see my business growing. I can see my family enjoying summer travel to places we've never been to.

I can see it because I know that I'm doing the one thing that helps achieve goals: dream them, determine the steps I need to take to achieve them—and then the hardest thing of all: exercise the determination to do the daily grind. This means doing the good, the bad and the ugly that needs to be done to achieve anything of significance.

There really is no secret to success other than doing the work. Making more and better art, as Seth Godin says. Or following your gut, as Danielle Laporte states. Or, my favorite quote from Marie Forleo: "If it's not a hell yeah! It's a no."

Self-reflection tools

Before you proceed to follow your dream, describe what success means to you. Remember, success is what *you* say it is. It's not what your parents tell you it is, or what your best friends think it is or what society at large defines it as. Success has many different faces, many different definitions. It could be securing a job at a specific company and getting paid a six-figure salary. It could be going back to college and getting your degree. It could be staying at home with your children. It could be volunteering in an underdeveloped country. It could be writing a book, launching a blog or establishing a business. The beauty of success is that it is for you to define. Once you've done that, then you have to roll up your sleeves. Yes, I believe in serendipity. I believe in happenstance. But I also believe that synchronicity is not going to follow you to the couch while you watch TV all day. Show up every day, do the work. Then success will find you!

Exercises

- Write down your definition of success. Know that definition may change over time. What is it for you now? It doesn't matter what others think. It's your life, it's your journey, it's your success.

- Face and deal with your FOMO (fear of missing out). Facebook, instagram, etc. give us access to what peers are doing and of course it always looks grand. Remember to stay true to your mission, to your heart and don't get sidetracked by comparisons and wanting to be everywhere at once.

- How can you be of service to others? If you keep your work mission-based it will resonate with others. A business that is only out there to make money, will only make money. It won't make a difference.

- Do more of what you are good at. Sharpen those skills, and delegate or just rule out those things you suck at. When you honor your true self, what you are here to do in life, you will thrive.

- Use the power of visualization. Whether you use a vision board, dream pillows or affirmations in a notebook, don't lose sight of your vision. See it and feel it unfold. That will keep you excited and energized, and help you do the drudgery work that is a part of any great endeavor.
- Realize we never "arrive" – what would you do if you lost everything today? What would your next endeavor be? What other projects would you love to launch? How can you branch out to your fullest potential?

Author Bio

At 45, Lorraine C. Ladish lost everything. In one big swoop she found herself separated from her husband, unemployed, broke, in huge debt, with two young daughters in tow. Just days from being homeless, she was forced to sell her family heirlooms to pay the rent. She had to apply for welfare and accept charity from friends and her daughters' school. With no job prospects in sight, she fell into a deep depression where there were days she couldn't get out of bed. During that time, she blogged. Success Diaries, written during the most difficult period of her life, was meant to help others find inspiration in life's small daily triumphs. But it also helped Lorraine pull herself out of a dark place. Within a year Success Diaries was published in Spain as a book: Diario del Exito.

Lorraine quickly recognized the power of the Internet and social media as a way to communicate and empower others. Within a few years, at the age of 50, she founded her company Viva Fifty Media LLC, the parent company of Viva Fifty! an online magazine that celebrates bicultural women 50+. The website started with a $500 investment. By bootstrapping and building a strong social media following, Viva Fifty! became profitable in less than a year, and became her sole source of income, surpassing what she used to earn as editor of other online publications.

Born into a family of writers, Lorraine C. Ladish (Madrid, 1963) is the author of 17 books that address women's issues, motherhood, and empowerment. She also published two novellas and is working on her third. From her early battle with bulimia to turning her life around in her late forties, Lorraine's books, blogs, articles and lectures are all about overcoming life's obstacles and motivating others. She is bicultural (U.S. and Spain), and is passionate about delivering her message of hope and empowerment in English and Spanish.

Resources

LorraineCLadish.com

VivaFifty.com

LatinaBloggersConnect.com

LatinasThinkBig.com

RedShoeMovement.com

LatinasInBusiness.us

BloggerBabes.com

BeBlogalicious.com

TheNetworkNiche.com

HispanicizEevent.com

TheAdelanteMovement.com

LATISM.org

SethGodin.com

DanielleLaporte.com

MarieForleo.com

100StartUp.com

I appreciate you!

And I really mean it.

Whoever you are, whether you know me in person or not, I'm sure you have a story, or more than one. We all do. I just hope that my journey will inspire you to realize that whatever type of success you want, is within your reach.

I'm a big believer in supporting one another, so if you liked this book, I would be extremely grateful if you wrote a review on Amazon, even if it's only two words: "liked it!"

You can also tweet about it and tag me at @lorrainecladish. I will always answer and retweet you! I'd love for you to connect with me on Facebook and Instagram and tell me how you found me through this book. You can also reach me at Lorraine@VivaFifty.com any time.

Here's wishing you much success, lots of it. The kind of success YOU want!

Warmly,

Lorraine